Mel Bay Presents Stefan Grossman's Guitar Workshop Video

Get Started On Guitar

By
Chet Atkins, cgp
& John Knowles

Complete DVD Learning System

THE GUITARISTS
Chet Atkins • Elizabeth Pearson • Will Mason

COVER PHOTO CREDIT
David Wolfram

DVD CREDITS

Executive Producer: Fred Kewley
Written and Produced by Chet Atkins and John Knowles
Directed by Ken Maxwell
Learning Design: Tom Sturdevant

1 2 3 4 5 6 7 8 9 0

Visit us on the Web at www.melbay.com — E-mail us at email@melbay.com

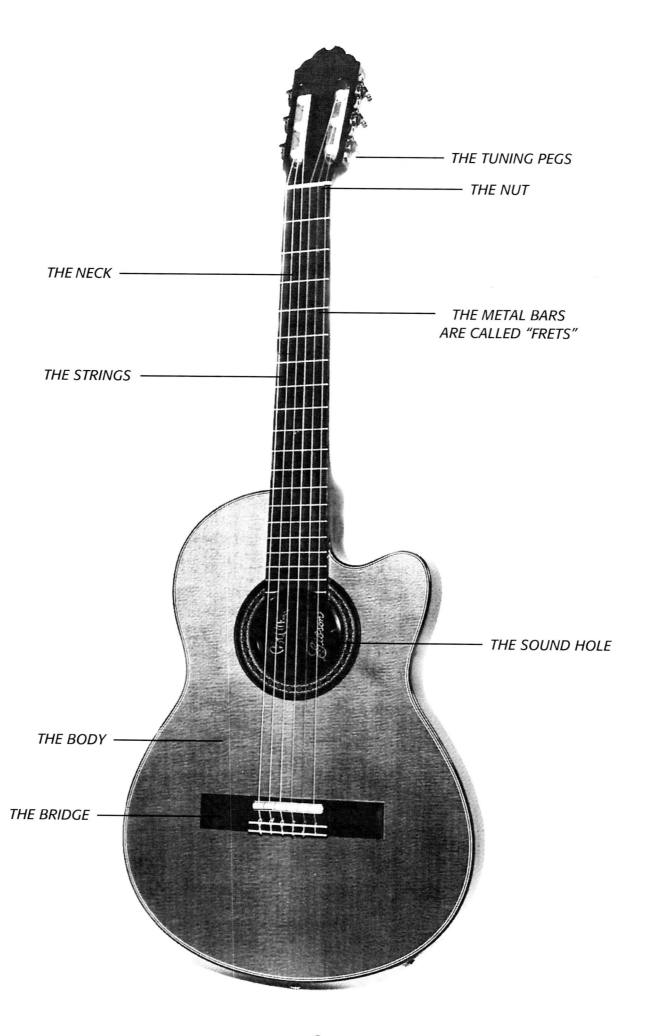

THE TUNING PEGS

THE NUT

THE NECK

THE METAL BARS
ARE CALLED "FRETS"

THE STRINGS

THE SOUND HOLE

THE BODY

THE BRIDGE

CONTENTS

THANKS...

In a project this big, there are a lot of people to thank like, Tom Sturdevant, Elizabeth Perdue Pearson, Will Mason, Darryl Dybka, Fred Kewley, Lauren Keiser, Gerry Teifer, Wesley Rose, Carolyn Campbell, Becky Knowles, Clyde Kendrick, Byron Fogo, Royce Jones, Tim Smith, Susan Hackney, Melodie Gimple, Kelly Force, Jo Motta, David Shookhoff, Slick Lawson, Susan Lawson, Steve O'Brien, Bruce Bolen, Randy Cullers, Pat Ledford, Ken Maxwell, Bob Hasentufel, Kendahl Maxwell, Jack Burns, Eddie Sloan, Scott Litteral, David Litteral, Paul Turner, Glenn Rieuf, David Hirsch, Bill Griffith, Mark Phillips, Pam Whittemore, Judy Komisky, Milt Okun.

This project is dedicated to

LENNY BREAU

(1941-1984)

INTRODUCTION

Photo: Slick Lawson

The first music I remember making was when, at the age of four or five, I inhaled and exhaled through a French harp. Those simple sounds were beautiful to my young ears. Later on, I graduated to the ukulele. As soon as I was large enough, I started playing guitar and quickly adapted to the two extra strings. I imitated everything I heard or saw musically and pretty soon was playing fairly well. We are all beginners at first, and I suppose we all learn by imitating. Listen to the beautiful sounds of the notes, learn to love them and pretty soon the guitar will become a great friend that you will want in your arms at all times. When that love affair begins, you can't help becoming a player. So learn everything you like in these lessons and remember that progress will be slow but sure.

Good luck! *Chet*

P. S. Dr. John Knowles is a dear friend and one of the smartest and best teachers I have seen work. There would be no book or video without him.

I was fourteen years old when I discovered Chet on a record. I knew right then that I wanted to play guitar like that. I remember thinking, "If he can do it...I can do it." I had taken piano lessons, and sung in the church choir, and I owned a ukulele. Most of all I wanted to make my own music. So I sat down, and I began listening... and playing along. It took me a while because I had never seen Chet and there was no book. I stuck with it... and every time I figured something out, I found several uses for it. Before long, it got easier... and I started to sound pretty good.

Things will be more or less the same for you. It is still a long road but Chet and I have done our best to pave it for you and provide you with maps. Your love of music and your desire to play the guitar are your best traveling companions. And all along the way there is the pure pleasure of making music... so let's GET STARTED! *John*

Photo: Slick Lawson

USING THIS BOOK

Throughout this book, you'll find DVD CHAPTER numbers that will help you link the text (and the music) to the video program. Each tune has its own section that includes basic information and advanced tips. Plus, there are special reference sections on PLAYING CHORDS, FINGERPICKING CHORDS, PLAYING MELODIES, and PLAYING BY EAR.

Photo: Melodie Gimple

What you see and hear, as you work through the book and DVD, will depend a lot on what you have learned so far. In the beginning, for example, you can use "IN TUNISIA" to tune your guitar. After a while, you will have learned enough to play the chords…and the melody.

THE BASICS BOX…

If you are new to the guitar, or if your strings have gotten a little rusty, follow the "BASICS BOX" to get started. As you go through the book and DVD, learning the basics of guitar playing, you will probably see and hear things you would like to try. Feel free to take the scenic route. Remember that you can turn the pages and pause the DVD whenever you like.

It's a good idea to begin each session by tuning up ("IN TUNISIA.") When you are ready, turn to the song you are working on and spend some time getting the feel of any new chords. Then turn on the DVD and play along with us. If you miss a chord, keep your place in the music so that you can come in on the next chord.

In most of the songs, you can repeat the chords you have learned for several verses. It is great practice to continue doing your part as we add a little fingerpicking… or a melody.

THE CLOCK…

You can use the clock in the upper right-hand corner of your screen to locate specific places within a DVD chapter. For example, if you would like to see how to play the C and G7 chords in "JAMBALAYA," go to **DVD CHAPTER 4** and fast-forward to **5:42**. You can locate specific verses in each tune using this same technique.

ON SCREEN CHORD SYMBOLS…

The name of each chord we play appears in the lower right corner of your screen. These symbols will refresh your memory as you play along with us.

IN TUNISIA

TUNING UP...

When you listen to "IN TUNISIA," you will hear the sound of each string. We begin with the first string, the high E. **(1:29)** If your guitar is close to being in tune, you can make minor adjustments as you listen. Remember that you can use your remote control to pause the DVD. You can also check your tuning during the other verses of "IN TUNISIA" since the chords and melody are built around the tuning sequence. As you listen to "IN TUNISIA," your ear for tuning will really improve.

MORE ABOUT TUNING...

Of course, there will be times when you will want to check your tuning without using the DVD. This is where tuning forks, pianos and electronic guitar tuners fit in.

The tuning fork has the advantage of being inexpensive and portable. An E (329.6) fork is a good choice because it sounds the same note as the open first string. Of course, you can find the same note on a piano but I've noticed that a piano is not quite as portable as a tuning fork.

Sound your E tuning fork on your knee or the heel of your shoe and touch the handle of the fork to the bridge of the guitar. You will hear the fork ring the note 'E.' Now sound the open E (first) string and listen. Is the string note higher... or lower... than the tuning fork note? Is it the same? Make a guess... and an adjustment. Are the two notes closer together?

This is the moment of truth, folks. If you listen carefully at this point you will get better and better at tuning. Listen for the sound of the fork to blend with the sound of the string as you adjust the first string. Take all the time you need.

Now let's check out the other strings. Sound your high E string. Keep that note in your ear... and press the second string at the fifth fret... and sound it. Do you hear the same note? You may need to adjust your second string. When you get it just right, the two strings together will sound almost like one big string.

Two down... four to go. Now you can use the second string to tune the third, the third to tune the fourth, and so on. Here is the step by step process along with a diagram that will help you remember how to tune.

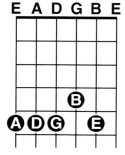

1. Tune the E (first) string to an E tuning fork.

2. Press the B (second) string at the fifth fret and tune it to the open E (first) string.

3. Press the G (third) string at the fourth fret and tune it to the open B string.

4. Press the D (fourth) string at the fifth fret and tune it to the open G string.

5. Press the A (fifth) string at the fifth fret and tune it to the open D string.

6. Press the E (sixth) string at the fifth fret and tune it to the open A string.

Now play the strings one at a time from high to low... and listen. Play a few chords... and listen. Are you satisfied? Take a moment to check any string that sounds suspicious.

There are almost as many ways to tune a guitar as there are ways to play one. You might have a piano handy and decide to get your 'E' from the E above middle C. You might want to invest in an electronic tuner. They are easy to use and pretty reliable.

The more you learn about tuning your guitar, the better you will sound when you play. In the beginning, you will tune so that it sounds good to your ear... and then your ear will improve. Before long, you will know a dozen ways to tune and be convinced that the factory put your frets in the wrong place.

THE G6 CHORD...

That G6 we play in "IN TUNISIA" is almost a G chord. The open first string helps the chord match the sound of the tuning. When you strum that next Em, stop at the second string and you will hear the B string. Strum through the chord progression G6, Em, G, D, Am, Em and listen for the tuning notes as you go. When you play along with "IN TUNISIA," you can alternate between checking your tuning and strumming the chords. **(2:29)**

G6

FINGERPICKING CHORDS...

We play a basic 'thumb, fingers, thumb, fingers' pattern in the fourth verse. **(3:29)** The chord progression with bass notes is,

CHORD NAME	G6	Em	G	D	Am	Em
BASS STRING	6	6	6	4	5	6

Did you notice that the last three bass notes are also tuning notes? What a coincidence.

You will usually get a good sound if you play the first three strings with your fingers. When we play "IN TUNISIA," we sound the second, third, and fourth strings on the Em and Am chords. It helps us hear the sound of the tuning. Here is a short sample that will get you ready to join us "IN TUNISIA."

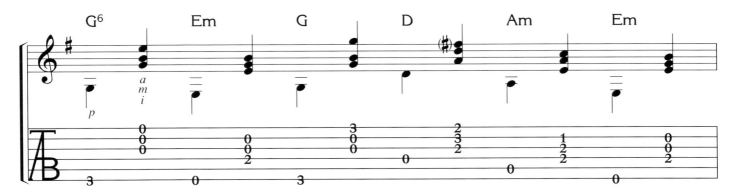

PLAYING THE MELODY...

The melody to "IN TUNISIA" was written around the tuning notes, E, B, G, D and A. I played the melody on the high strings in the third verse **(2:59)** and on the low strings in the fifth verse **(3:58)**. Here is a guide to the location of the tuning notes.

There are some clues to other melodies in these tuning notes. "KNUCKLEBUSTERS" and "NEW GUITAR BLUES" also come from this set of notes. You could start with these notes and make up some of your own fills to these tunes.

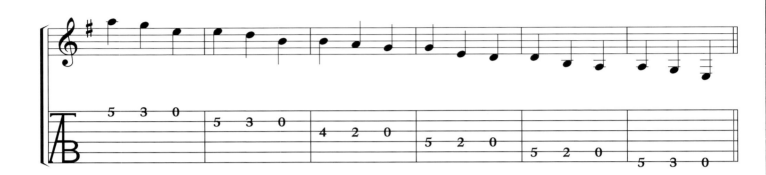

SPECIAL EFFECTS...

The tuning notes come up again in the lick I played at the end of "IN TUNISIA." **(DVD CHAPTER 25)** Practice playing the first six notes of the lick to get the pattern down. The whole lick is three groups of six plus one note to end on.

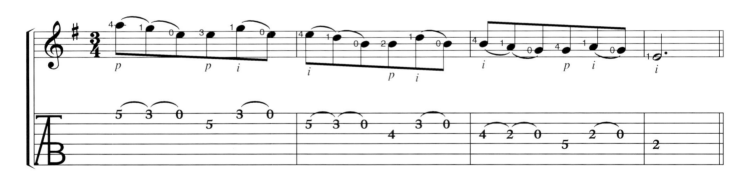

IN TUNISIA

by John Knowles

(1:55)

No chord (N.C.)

One,   two,   one two   three four

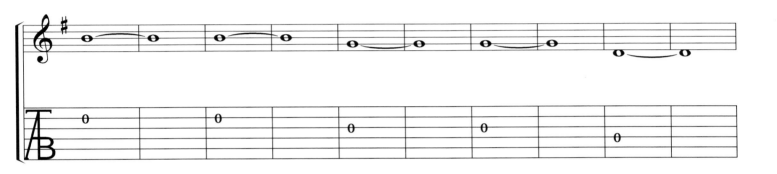

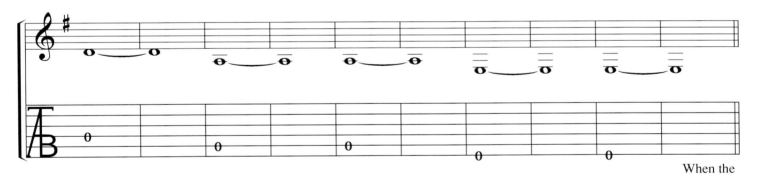

When the

(2:29) G6   G6   Em   Em

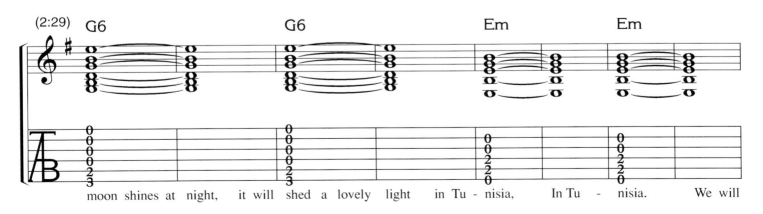

moon shines at night,   it will shed a lovely   light   in Tu - nisia,   In Tu - nisia.   We will

sit beneath the stars strummin' chords on our gui-tars, in Tu - nisia, in Tu - nisia. Where I

want to go, ask me why but I don't know, in Tu - nisia, in Tu - nisia.

(2:59)

10

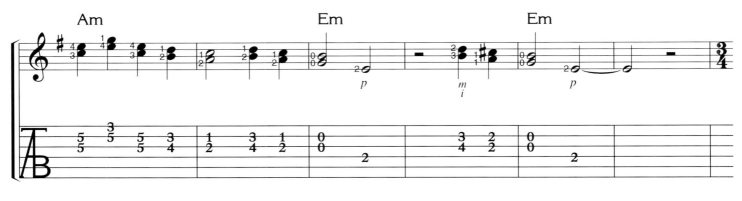

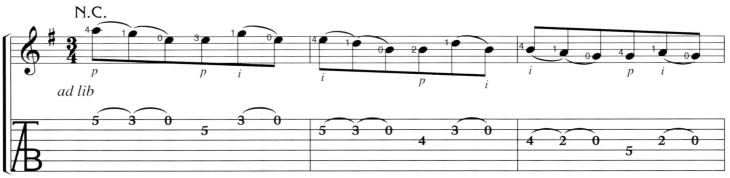

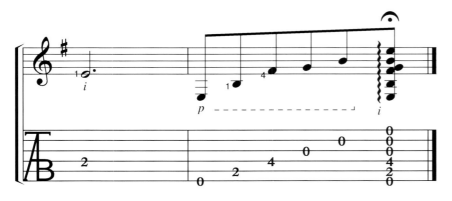

14

JAMBALAYA

C AND G7 CHORDS...

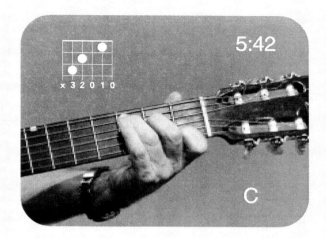

This one is a two-chord classic. We start it in the key of C with a C chord and a G7 chord. **(5:39)** In Nashville, players call chords by numbers. In the key of C, C is called the 1 chord because it is built on the first note in the scale. G7 is called the 5 chord because G is five notes up the scale (C, D, E, F, G).

Place your fingertips on the strings in the pattern of the C chord. **(DVD CHAPTER 26)** Relax your hand so you are barely touching the strings. The sound of the strings is probably muffled. Now press the strings down to the fingerboard... and release... and press ... and release... you can feel the shape of the chord. Sound each note in the chord and adjust your fingers to get a clear tone from each string. I get the best sound, with the least effort, when the tip of each finger is close to the metal fret.

When you make a C chord, your fingertips are very close to a G7 chord. If you look at the shift diagram, you will see where each finger goes when you change from C to G7. Your first finger moves

from the second string to the first string. Practice moving your first finger without moving the others. Then move your second and third fingers together without moving your first finger. When you are ready, move all three fingers from C... to G7. Now release... shift... press... and you are back on C.

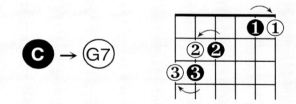

You can use these two chords to play the first verse and chorus of "JAMBALAYA." **(7:09)** The music sample below shows six measures taken from the intro to "JAMBALAYA." The count and the lyrics will help you feel the timing of the chord changes. We strum the G7 on the word *"gun"* and the C chord on the word *"bayou."* Singing the melody will help you feel the time and hear the chord changes.

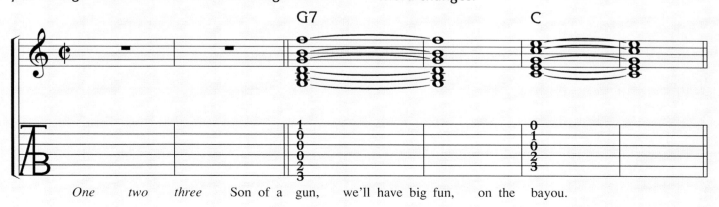

One   two   three   Son of a gun,   we'll have big fun,   on the   bayou.

15

G and D7 Chords...

It would be fun to learn a few more chords and play all of "JAMBALAYA." In the second verse and chorus, we go to the key of G where G is the 1 chord and D7 is the 5 chord. **(6:05)** When you change from G to D7, your third finger moves from the sixth string to the first string. Your second finger moves from the fifth string to the third. When you practice this move, hold on with your fourth finger to guide your second and third fingers into place. On your way back to G, hold on with your first finger to help 2 and 3 find their way. **(7:59)**

D and A7 Chords...

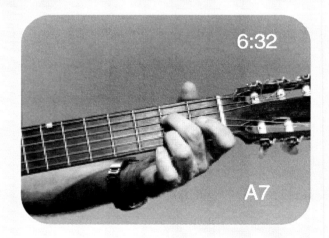

Once you know a few chords, it gets easier to learn new ones. D and A7 are the 1 chord and the 5 chord in the key of D. **(6:22)** I am using fingering that makes it easy for me to shift from D to A7 and back again. Notice that the first and second fingers keep their shape as I shift back and forth. I don't always use this fingering for A7. In fact, I have learned several ways to do almost everything... and I am always choosing the way that feels best at the moment. **(8:42)**

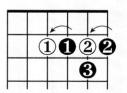

A and E7 Chords...

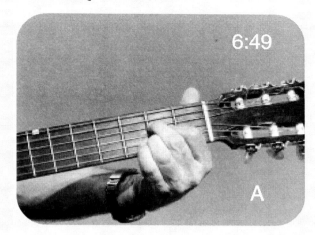

The last verse and chorus of "JAMBALAYA" are in the key of A. **(6:44)** You might have guessed that A is the 1 chord, E7 is the 5. I use this fingering for the A chord because my first finger just slides back a fret when I shift to E7. **(9:25)**

At this point, you have learned eight chords. If you check out the chord chart at the back of the book you will see that you have learned over half of the chords it takes to play along with all the songs on the DVD. Of course, there is a lot more to learn about the guitar and its music, but if anyone asks... tell them you are a guitar player.

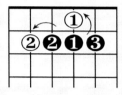

ALTERNATING BASS...

We use the 'thumb, fingers, thumb, fingers' move in "JAMBALAYA" to get an alternating bass-line going. **(DVD CHAPTER 27)** Make a C chord and sound the fifth string with your thumb. Then sound the first three strings with your fingers. Now shift your third finger (left hand) to the sixth string, third fret. This is the alternate bass note. Sound the sixth string with your thumb, and then sound your fingers on the first three strings. Your third finger (left hand) and thumb (right hand) move back and forth to alternate the bass note. The rest of the chord stays the same. You probably noticed that the fourth string is fretted but not sounded. You can relax your second finger if you like.

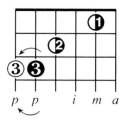

Here is the alternating bass pattern for a C and a G7 written out in music notation and TAB. When you play alternate bass on a G7, your thumb moves between the sixth and fourth strings. The left hand fingering stays the same.

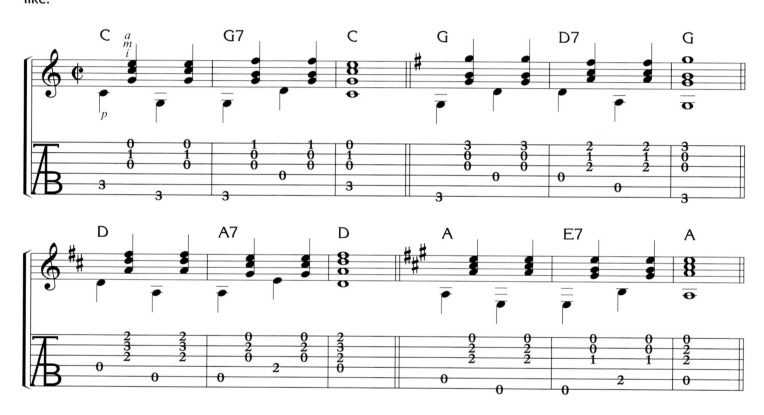

You might have noticed that it is easier to read the music and TAB than it is to read all the explanations and follow the chord diagrams. Chord diagrams do a great job when your left hand is holding still. When things start to move, like in fingerpicking and melody playing, the music and TAB seem to work better. You can use all of this and your ear in whatever way helps you become a better guitar player and musician.

Now you can try this out on the first verse of "JAMBALAYA." We start the alternating pattern in the chorus but you can play it during the verse while we are strumming the chords. **(7:38)** If you knew which strings to sound with your thumb, you could play this alternating bass pattern on all of "JAMBALAYA." I played through all of these patterns on the DVD. **(DVD CHAPTER 27)**

JAMBALAYA

DVD CHAPTER 5

written by Hank Williams

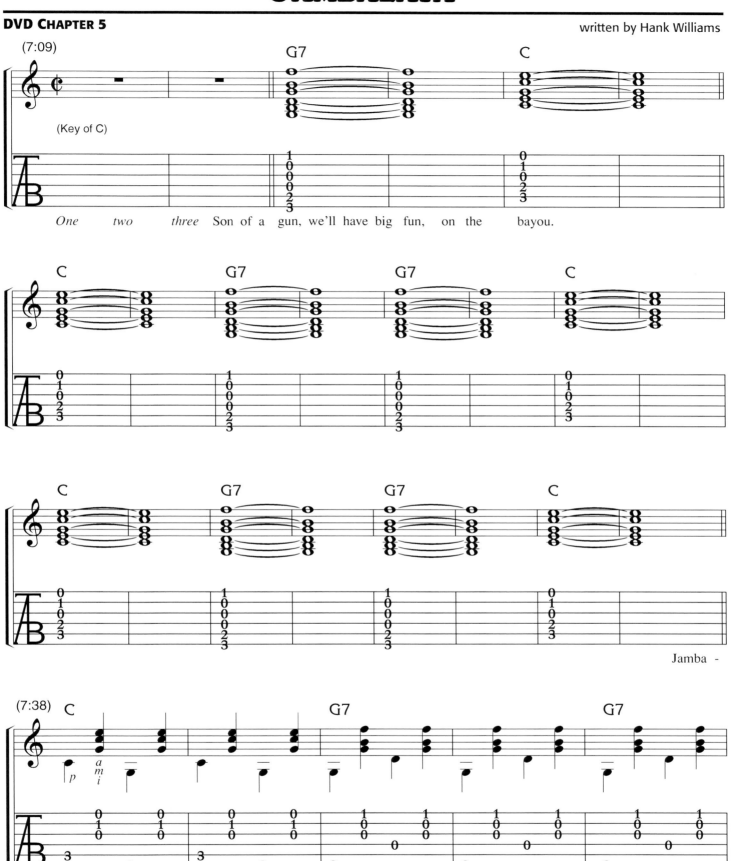

see my ma cher a - mi - o.   Pick gui - tar,   fill fruit jar   and be

gay - o.   Son of a gun, we'll have big fun   on the   bayou.

(7:59)

(Key of G)

(8:21)

20

21

Goodbye

(9:25)
(Key of A)

Joe, me gotta go, meoh myoh.   Me gotta   go,   pole the   pirogue down the bayou.   My Y-

vonne, the sweetest one,   meoh   myoh.   Son of a gun, we'll have big   fun   on the   bayou.

(9:46)

ON TOP OF OLD SMOKY

1, 4 AND 5 CHORDS...

You already know all of the chords that we use to play "OLD SMOKY." It takes three chords to play each verse. We start in the key of G with G, C and D7. **(10:18)** You might remember that we called G the 1 chord and D7 the 5 chord. Since C is the fourth note in a G scale, let's call C the 4 chord in the key of G.

Let's take a look at the shift from G to C and back. It feels a lot like the C to G7 shift because the second and third fingers hold their shape. **(11:45)**

After three verses of "OLD SMOKY," we change to the key of D. **(10:57)** Now G is the 4 chord and A7 is the 5. The only new shift is from D to G and back. Again, your second and third fingers can hold their shape so that the move will go smoothly. By the way... have you been singing along as you play the chords? **(12:53)**

For the last three verses of "OLD SMOKY," we modulate to the key of A. **(11:17)** Now D is the 4 chord and E7 is the 5. Here is a chart that shows how the chords work in each key.

	1	4	5
KEY OF G	G	C	D7
KEY OF D	D	G	A7
KEY OF A	A	D	E7

Examine the diagram for the shift between A and D. Notice that your third finger works like a sliding anchor to guide your other fingers into place. **(13:56)**

What would happen if you changed chords with your eyes closed? Now is as good a time as any to see what happens. The more you play the guitar, the more your fingers know their way around.

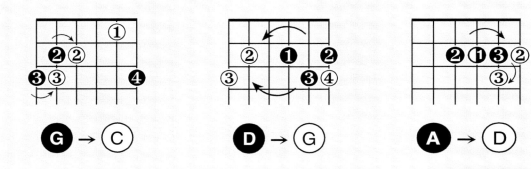

FINGERPICKING CHORDS...

The alternating bass pattern that we use in "ON TOP OF OLD SMOKY" is similar to the pattern that we used in "JAMBALAYA." Since "SMOKY" is in 3/4 time, we play 'thumb, fingers, fingers' so that everything fits a three count. You'll notice that we don't always alternate the bass. Almost any pattern is more interesting if you throw in a little variety.

We play this pattern in verse 2 in the key of G, **(12:11)** verse 5 in the key of D, **(13:14)** and verse 8 in the key of A. **(14:17)** You can use it on all of the verses. It will sound good as long as you are in the right key.

PLAYING THE MELODY...

When we played the backup to "SMOKY," we used a 'bass–chord–chord' pattern to fit the 3/4 time. **(12:11)** That bass note on the downbeat helps you feel the beginning of each measure. You can go for that same feel when you play the melody.

Here is a sample of the melody to "SMOKY" in the key of G. All of the notes have been converted to quarter notes. There are three in each measure. As you play this sample, emphasize (>) the first note in each measure and you will feel the 3/4 timing.

Now play a little of the melody like I played it on the DVD. **(12:32)** We play the first three verses in the key of G. You can play melody behind our singing for two verses and then join me in the third. Adjust your melody to match our singing. That way each verse will have its own feel.

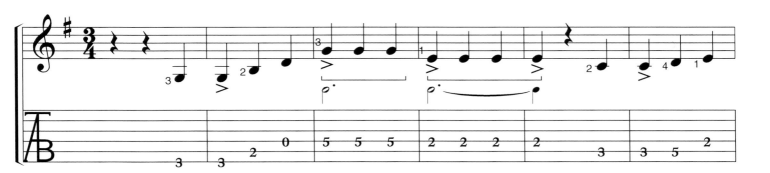

ADDING HARMONY TO MELODIES...

You can dress up a melody by tossing in some of the chords you already know. When I played the melody to "SMOKY" in the key of D, I used the Am chord to season my solo. **(13:35)** I played the Am shape, two frets higher than normal to get a Bm harmony. I moved it down, one fret at a time, and then played three open strings, which gives a G harmony. Here are four diagrams that show the move. I used my thumbpick to sound the second, third, and fourth strings. You could use p, i, m.

I used familiar chords to dress up the melody in "NEW GUITAR BLUES" and "KNUCKLEBUSTERS." I often use parts of chords to add a little harmony to a melody.

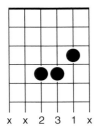
x x 2 3 1 x

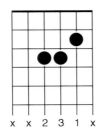
x x 2 3 1 x

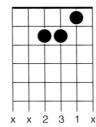
x x 2 3 1 x

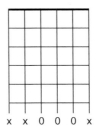
x x 0 0 0 x

On Top of Old Smoky

arranged by Chet Atkins and John Knowles

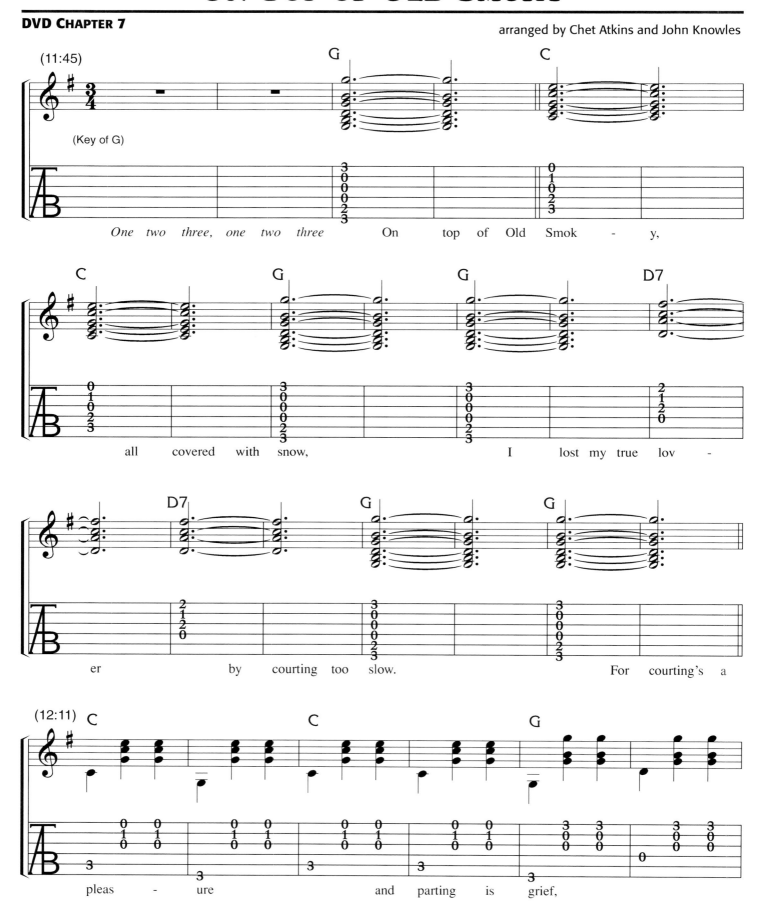

but a false hearted lov - - - er   is   worse than a

thief.

A   thief will just

rob   you   and take what you save,   but a false hearted

lov - er   will lead you to the grave.   The grave will de-

vour   you   and turn you to   dust.

Not a girl in a   hun - - dred   that a   poor boy can

trust.

They'll tell you they

love you and tell you more lies than crossties on a

rail - road or stars in the sky. On top of Old

Smok - - - y, all covered with snow,

I lost my true lov - - - er

29

by courting too slow.

Photo: Melodie Gimple

NEW GUITAR BLUES

B7 CHORD...

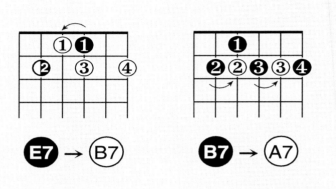

The traditional blues progression uses the 1, 4 and 5 chords. **(15:03)** All of the chords are played as seventh chords. The only new chord in this one is B7. Make a B7... lift your fourth finger and you will notice that the other fingers make the shape of a D7 chord. Sometimes I play B7 without using my fourth finger. It works as long as I am careful not to sound the first string when I strum.

Let's look at the shifting pattern for going from E7 to B7. **(DVD CHAPTER 28)** Practice keeping your second finger in place while you move your first finger. This second finger 'anchor' will really improve your accuracy. When you make the complete shift, set your third and fourth fingers at the same time as you move your first finger.

Now make a B7... and lift your first and fourth fingers. Do you recognize the shape of the A7 chord in your second and third fingers? Now hold on to that shape and shift to A7. When we shifted to A7 from D in "JAMBALAYA," we ended up with a different fingering. Remember what I said about learning several ways to do everything and choosing the best one for the situation.

We use these three chords to play the first verse of "NEW GUITAR BLUES," but you can keep going through the whole song. These chords will sound just fine with the blues licks that we play in the other verses. **(16:44)**

BLUES LICK #1...

Will demonstrates a blues lick **(15:48)** that we use in the second, fourth and sixth verses of the "BLUES." There is a pattern for each chord in the tune. These diagrams will give you the finger positions. You can get the timing by playing along with us.

I pick two strings at once with my thumb pick. Elizabeth and Will used flatpicks to play these licks.

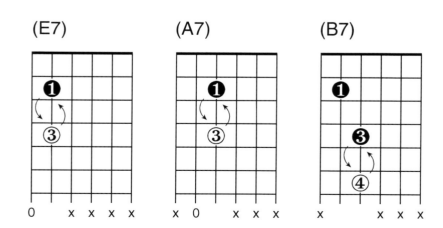

32

BLUES LICK #2...

Listen to Elizabeth demonstrate this lick **(16:14)** and you will notice that the timing of the two blues licks is the same. I'll give you one measure of TAB for the 1, 4 and 5 chords so that you can get the fingering. Then you can join us in the third, fifth, and seventh verses.

PLAYING THE MELODY...

If you're going to play the blues, you've got to bend the notes. I bend the first note of my first solo in the "BLUES." **(18:11)** I fret the first string at the sixth fret and push it toward the second string. I pick the string just as I bend it. I have learned how far to push it to get a note that is close to the B at the seventh fret.

This is written in the TAB as 6 (7).

Sometimes I push the string before I pick it and then relax the bend to get a note that goes down.

This is written in the TAB as (8) 7.

Play around with bending the notes to get a sound like a person singing. You'll notice that I bend the notes in a lot of my solo playing. You can use it whenever you think it fits.

A steel string bends further than a nylon string. If you are playing on nylon strings, you might try replacing some of the bends with slides. When you see 2 (3), just slide your finger from the second fret to the third fret as you think blues.

ADDING HARMONY TO MELODY...

I used an old blues move that is based on a Dm chord shape in my first solo. **(18:30)** I started up on the seventh fret and worked my way down to the third fret. The roman numerals on the diagrams tell you the fret numbers for chords up the neck. The first three chords go with the B7 chord. The next three go with the A7.

(B7)   (A7)

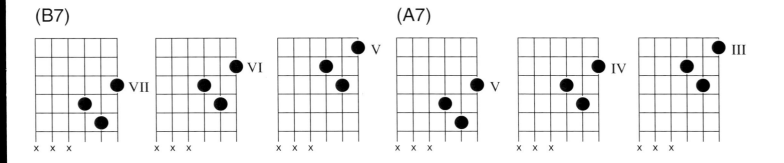

33

New Guitar Blues

by Chet Atkins and John Knowles

One two three four, One two three I laid down my last dollar, bought myself a new gui-

tar. I laid down my last dollar, bought myself a new gui - tar.

Got big plans for the future, someday I'll be a star. Been

playin' 'bout a week now, seems more like seven days.

bone.   My   calouses have blisters,

my folks have all left   home.

(18:11)

I met a

I played the blues in E, I thought she'd be im-

pressed. She said, "Goodbye, please don't call me."

You don't want to hear the rest.

Somewhere in this old world, there's a man I'm lookin' for.

Somewhere in this old world, there's a man I'm lookin' for.

He's got to sing the blues

and maybe own a music store.

(20:02)

39

Dm AND Am CHORDS...

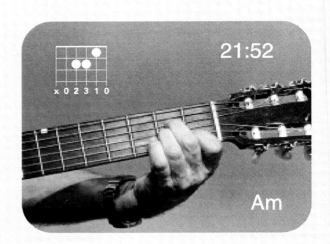

By now, you are probably getting the feel of shifting from one chord to another in one smooth motion. Let's add a couple of minor chords to the chords we already know. **(21:45)**

In "PLAYING FOR SCALE," we shift from C to Dm. Your first and second fingers keep their shape as you shift. You can make a C chord... lift your third finger... shift your first and second finger... and set your fourth finger in place... and you're on Dm. **(DVD CHAPTER 29)**

When you shift from Dm to G7, hang on to your first finger. That 'anchor' finger will help your other

fingers find their way. As you learn new chords, you will find fingers that can serve as guides from one chord to another.

There are two anchors in the shift from C to Am. Your third finger is the only finger that moves. Let your first and second fingers give a little as you shift so that each chord has its own feel.

Shifting from Am to Dm is a lot like shifting from C to Dm. You release your third finger and keep the shape of your first and second fingers as you shift. **(21:58)**

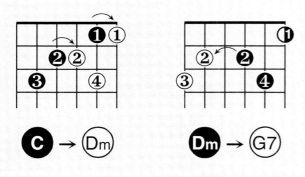

C → Dm   Dm → G7

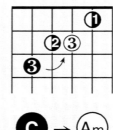

C → Am

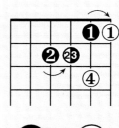

Am → Dm

PLAYING THE SCALE...

The scale tune is a good place to begin teaching your fingers and your ears to play melody. A lot of beautiful melodies have been written from the scale. **(20:36)**

Here is the scale that Elizabeth and Will played on the DVD. The fingering that Elizabeth called out is written above each note. The alphabet names that Will called are written below each note.

The TAB shows you where to find each note on the guitar. The top line of the TAB represents the high E (first) string. The numbers on each line are fret numbers. The scale passage starts with a 'G' on the first string at the third fret and ends with a 'C' on the fifth string at the third fret. All of the music in the book is written out this way.

As you play the first verse of "PLAYING FOR SCALE," let your left-hand fingers step from one note to the next. You want the sound of one note to connect smoothly to the sound of the next note.

I use an alternating right-hand finger pattern to sound the scale notes. **(23:42)** As I play a note with my index finger, my middle finger gets ready to play the next note… like walking across the strings.

On the DVD, Will plays the melody from the first verse while I play the second verse. The third and fourth verses fit together in the same way. As I play the fourth verse, Elizabeth repeats the melody from the third verse.

FINGERPICKING CHORDS...

Will and Elizabeth took turns playing a finger-style backup to the scales. I played a brief excerpt from their accompaniment on the DVD. **(DVD CHAPTER 29)**

The sample below is based on the four chord progression they played. You can use it to get the pattern in your fingers and then join us on the DVD.

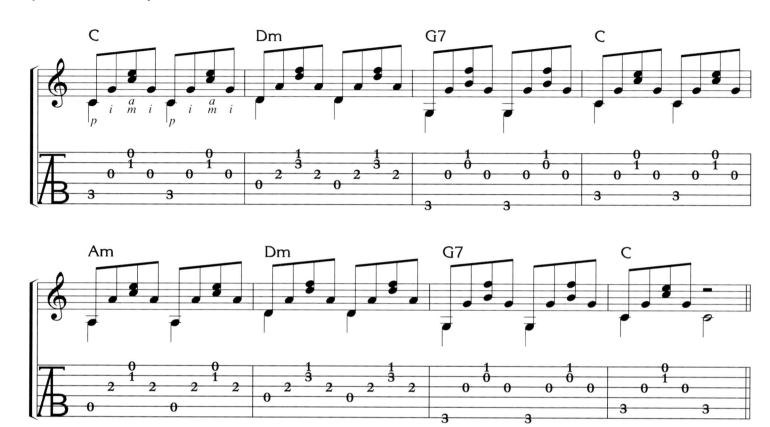

SPECIAL EFFECTS...

In the last verse of "PLAYING FOR SCALE," I played some harmonics mixed in with regular notes to create the melody. **(25:13)** To make a harmonic, I touch the string with my index finger just as I pick it with my thumb. The trick is to touch the string exactly twelve frets up from where the left hand is fretting. In the

example below, I play all open strings so the harmonics are produced by touching the string at the twelfth fret. **(DVD CHAPTER 30)**

The harmonics are indicated in the TAB by asterisks under the fret numbers. I use my ring finger (a) to play the regular notes.

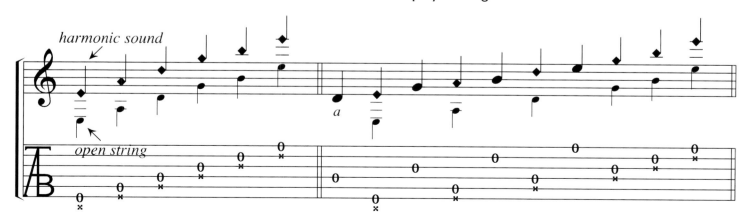

Playing For Scale

by John Knowles

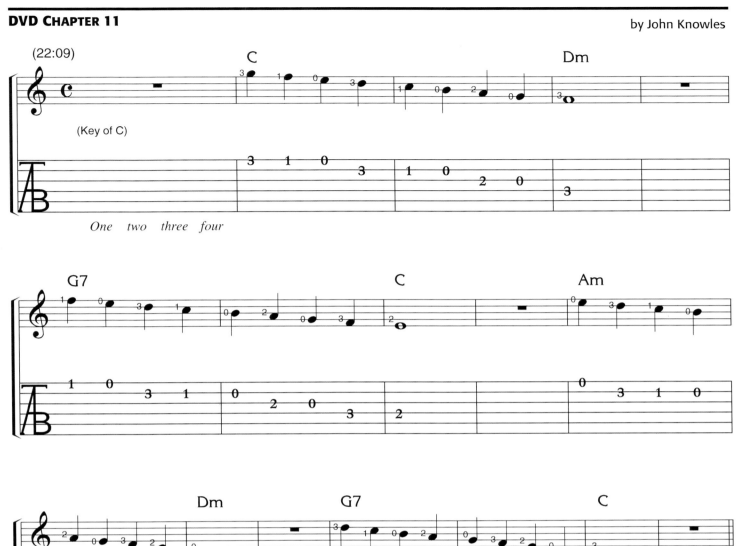

(22:09)

(Key of C)

One two three four

(22:57)

44

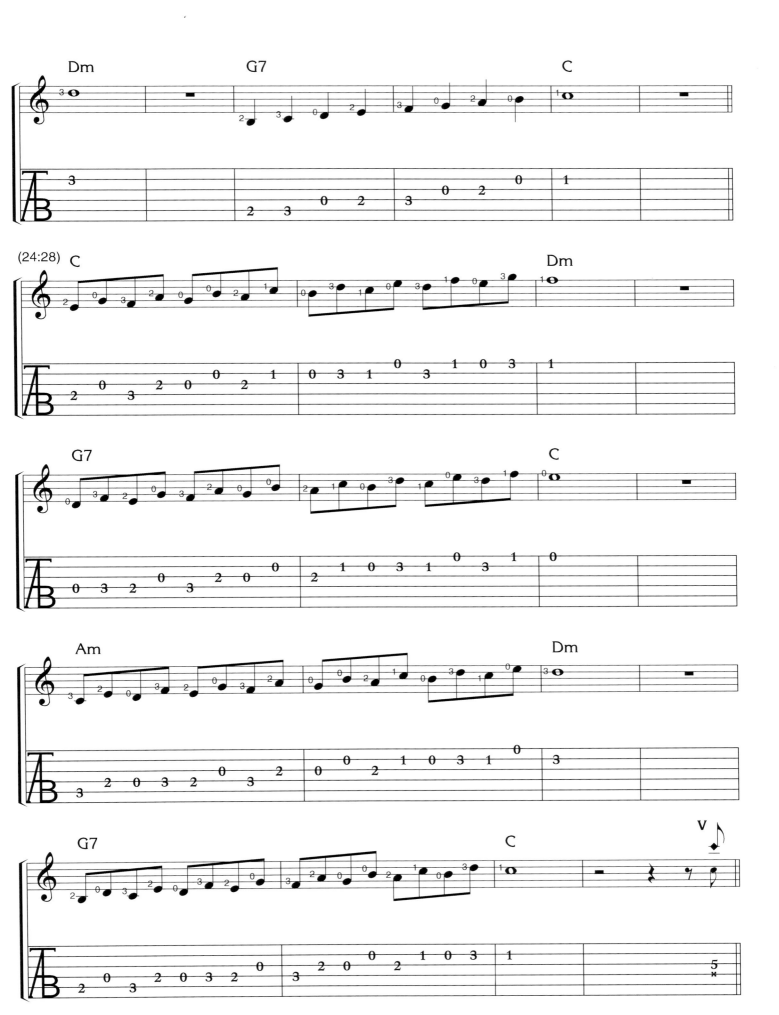

TAKE ME HOME, COUNTRY ROADS

Em AND F CHORDS...

In the verses, there is a shift from a G chord to an Em. Your second finger makes a great anchor on the fifth string. The Em then changes to a D chord. It may help you to notice that your second finger stays on the same fret as it moves across the fingerboard from the fifth string to the first string. Your second finger can guide the rest of your fingers into place. You can play all of the verses and choruses with G, Em, D and C. **(26:53)**

I noticed that Elizabeth uses a four string version of Em that only takes one finger to make... and it really sets up the shift to F. Do you see how your second finger guides the other fingers into place? Let your first finger lie down and cover two strings to make the F chord. Your second and third fingers remain standing so that they will touch only one string each.

When you shift from F to C, your first finger works like a moving anchor. It stands up on the second string. Keep the shape in your second and third fingers as they move into position. Now you can join us for the bridge. **(28:38)**

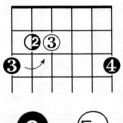

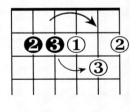

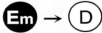

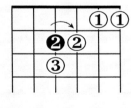

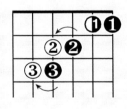

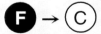

A NEW FINGERPICKING PATTERN...

In "TAKE ME HOME, COUNTRY ROADS," we combined two of the basic moves to create a new right hand pattern. **(26:26)** Elizabeth uses it in the intro **(26:53)** and again in the second verse and chorus. **(27:50)** Here's a sample that used the chord progression from the chorus.

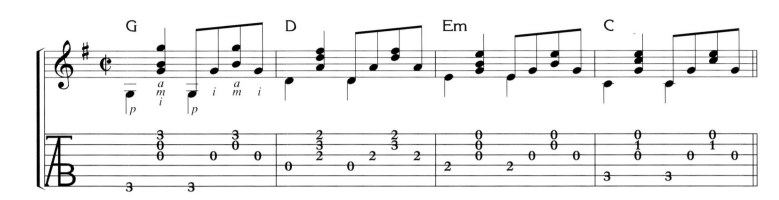

Photo: Melodie Gimple

48

Take Me Home, Country Roads

by Bill Danoff, Taffy Nivert and John Denver

Country

long.　　　　　　　　　　West Vir - ginia,

mountain　momma,　　　　　　　　　take me

home,　　　　　country　roads,　　　　　Take me

home,　　　　　country　roads,　　　　take me home,

country　roads.

YESTERDAY

B7sus AND Am7 CHORDS...

There are a couple of variations on familiar chords in our version of this classic Beatles tune. The diagrams show how to finger the B7sus ('sus' is shorthand for suspended 4th) and the Am7. When you strum the B7sus, let your second finger lean against the fifth string. This will keep the fifth string from sounding.

The shift from G to B7sus and the shift from B7sus to B7 are shown in the diagrams below.

We play all three of these chords without sounding the first string. It makes the shifting smoother and it fits the right hand fingerpicking pattern that we use. As you watch the DVD, you may notice that Will leaves out fingers in several other chords.

We play "YESTERDAY" with a capo on the second fret. The fingering is regular 'G' fingering, but the sound is higher. A capo is great for adjusting your guitar to fit your voice. **(30:07)**

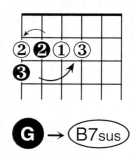

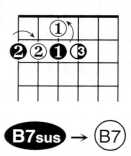

FINGERPICKING CHORDS...

Our arrangement of "YESTERDAY" really shows the advantage of playing chords fingerstyle. In the first verse Will is making parts of chords with his left hand. **(31:14)** He begins with a one-finger G chord. He can get away with using only one finger because he is skipping the first and fifth strings. Here are some chord diagrams that will give you the feel of letting some fingers rest while your right hand skips strings. You will find that this way of playing chords comes naturally after you have worked out several tunes, step by step.

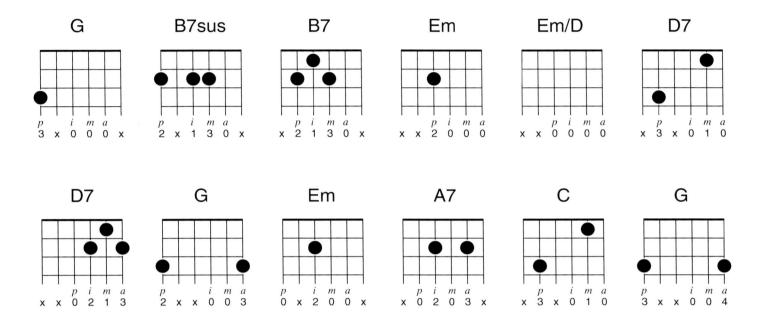

57

YESTERDAY

by John Lennon and Paul McCartney

(Key of G fingering; Capo 2 — Key of A)

One two three four

Yesterday

life was such an easy game to play. Now I need a place to

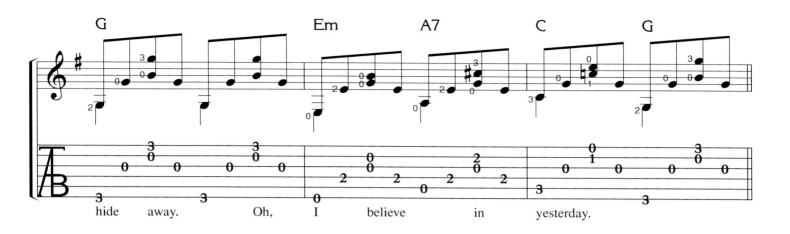

hide   away.   Oh,   I   believe   in   yesterday.

(31:55)

Why   she (he)   had to go,   I don't   know,   she (he)   wouldn't

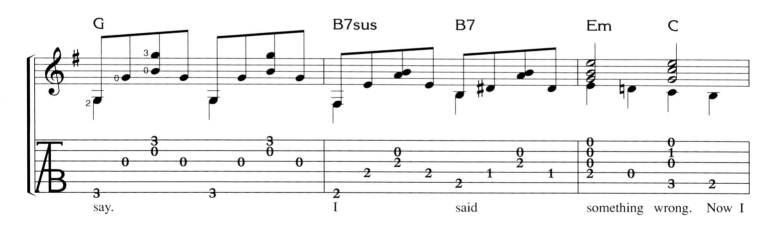

say.   I   said   something wrong. Now I

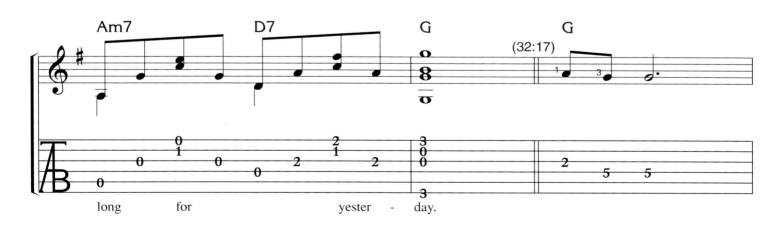

(32:17)

long   for   yester - day.

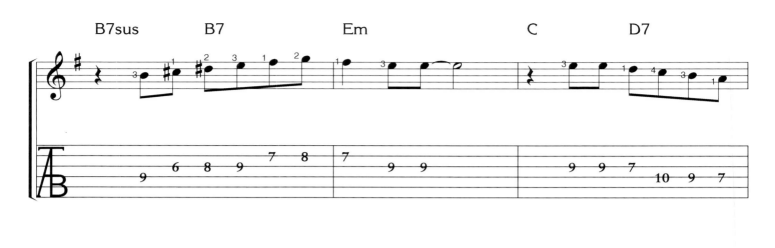

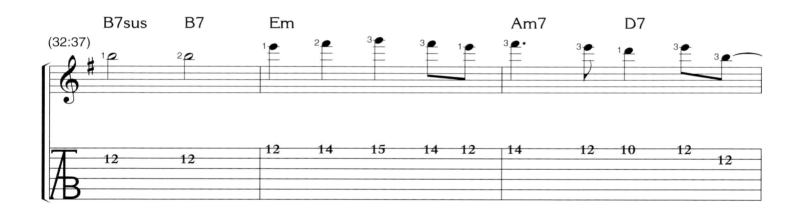

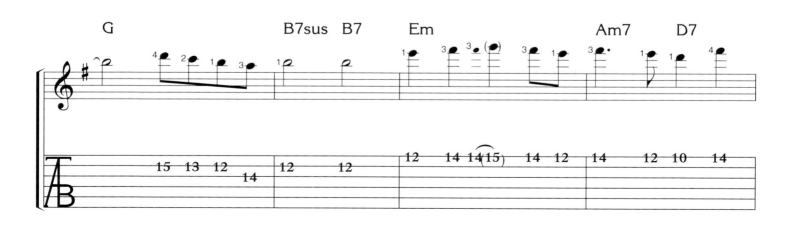

GREENSLEEVES

Congratulations...

You know all of the chords it takes to play along with us on "GREENSLEEVES." As a matter of fact, you could play along with the whole DVD now. While you're strumming, you may hear a melody you'd like to learn, or notice a right hand rhythm pattern that you could use. Who knows?

WILL'S SOLO...

You can learn a lot about timing from Will's solo. The bass drum is sounding on the beat. Four beats make up one bar or measure of music. In 4/4 time, a quarter note (♩), lasts for one beat. When you tap your finger along with the bass drum beat, you are tapping quarter notes. Can you tap your way through Will's solo and get to the end of the written music at the same time he finishes playing? **(35:42)**

The names of the other notes give big hints about how timing works. Is it any surprise that a half note (♩) lasts as long as two quarter notes? Don't you think that a whole note (o) should last as long as two half notes? When a note is followed by a dot, it gets its regular time plus half its regular time. For example, a dotted half note (♩.) is worth two quarters... plus one quarter. Here is a list of notes that shows how much time to give to each kind of note.

TIMING THE NOTES

QUARTER	♩ =	♩
HALF	♩ =	♩ + ♩
DOTTED HALF	♩. =	♩ + ♩ + ♩
DOTTED HALF	o =	♩ + ♩ + ♩ + ♩

Here is a sample from Will's "GREENSLEEVES" solo. All of the notes have been converted to quarter notes so that you play on every bass drum beat. Play it this way and then play it like Will does and you will really start to feel the timing. You can learn a lot from playing around with music like this. Of course, you already know a lot just from listening to the music.

(Bass drum)

FINGERPICKING CHORDS...

Elizabeth uses a variation on a familiar pattern to back up my solo. She adjusted the "PLAYING FOR SCALE/YESTERDAY" pattern to fit 3/4 time. Here is a sequence you can work out to get you started on "GREENSLEEVES." Notice that we are still using chord names for bass notes. **(34:48)**

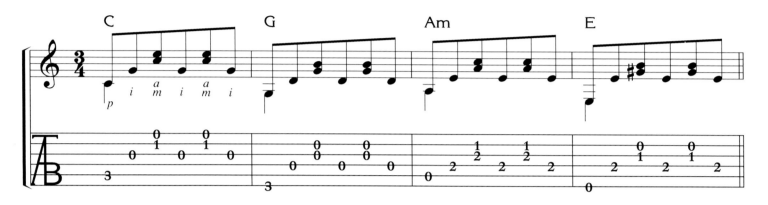

ELIZABETH'S SOLO...

You can create a nice accompaniment to a melody by playing a bass line. The safest bass note is… you guessed it… the chord name. Elizabeth's solo in "GREENSLEEVES" is a good example of this approach. **(33:49)** There are four chords in our arrangement and that gives us our four bass notes.

Here is an exercise that is based on "GREENSLEEVES." Hold on with your third finger so that the bass notes will ring under the melody. Play the bass notes with your thumb and the melody

notes with your fingers. Your ear will fill in the harmony that is suggested by the bass notes.

There are three things you can do to learn Elizabeth's solo. First play the melody along with her. The stems of the melody point up. (♩) Then play the bass part (stems pointing down) without the melody. (℗) Finally… melody and bass together. After you can play both parts together, go back and play them alone. This will help you keep the bass and melody separate in your mind… and the listener's ear.

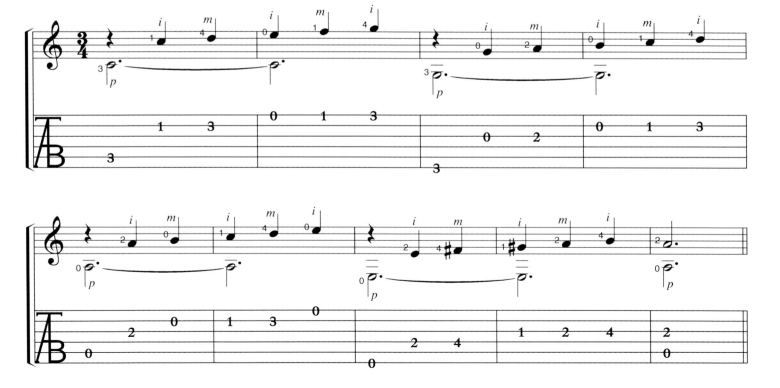

GREENSLEEVES

arranged by Chet Atkins and John Knowles

One two three, one two   (Elizabeth)

65

66

68

PICKIN' PRODUCE

DVD CHAPTER 18

In "PICKIN' PRODUCE" I keep time with my thumb and play melody with my fingers. **(37:27)** It's the same thing that piano players do with two hands. I use a thumb pick and I rest my hand lightly on the strings at the bridge to get a sound that complements the melody. **(DVD CHAPTER 32)** I have heard other players get a similar effect without a thumb pick. Let your ear help you find a way.

The tune is in the key of A and there are three chords. They are A, D and E7, the 1, 4 and 5 chords. The bass notes alternate like in the 'boom chic' pattern we played in "JAMBALAYA." Here is a little bit of TAB to show you the thumb pattern for each chord. When you are ready, turn on the DVD and give your thumb a chance to keep time.

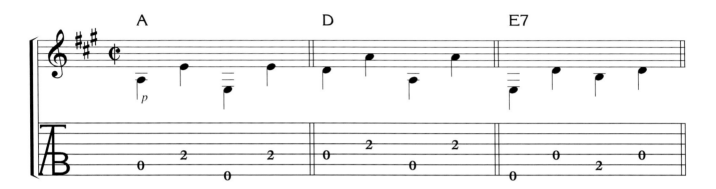

Once you get your thumb going, you will want to throw in a few notes with your fingers. The *"Beans…"* section of the piece will help you get a feel for timing your fingers with your thumb. **(38:45)** For starters, make an A chord, get your thumb going, and just sing *"Beans… Beans…"* with Will and Elizabeth. (Make sure no one is watching or be prepared to explain yourself.) As you get the feel of it, your fingers will join in when you sing the vegetables.

Most of the rhythms in the other tunes I played in "PICKIN' PRODUCE" are combinations of the rhythms

of those four vegetables. "CAMPTOWN RACES" is *"Rutabaga, Turnip Greens, Okra, Okra."* Toss in a few vegetables of your own if you need to.

Sometimes I play a melody note slightly ahead of the bass note. It relaxes the feel and makes it sound more like two guitars. You can practice this on *"Pickin' Produce all day long."* Play it straight until you get to *"day."* Then come in just a bit early on the third-string melody note.

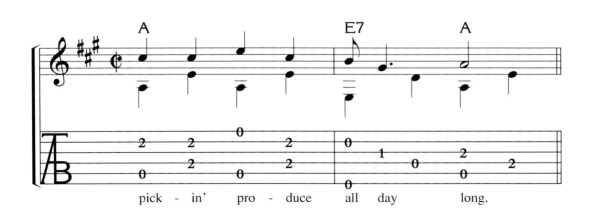

pick - in' pro - duce all day long.

PICKIN' PRODUCE

by Chet Atkins and John Knowles

Up at sun-up, work till sun-down,

pick-in' pro-duce all day long.

(CAMPTOWN RACES)

71

Doo - dah,　　doo - dah.

Pick - in' pro - duce all day long.

(39:58)

(AUNT RHODY)

Pick - in' pro - duce all day long.

(40:15)

(O SUSANNA)

Pick - in' pro - duce all day long.

(GOIN' HOME)

(STARS AND STRIPES)

73

Up at sun - up, work till sun - down, pick - in' pro - duce all day long.

74

Corn,   egg - plant,

ar - ti - choke,   gua - ca - mo - le.   Pick - in' pro - duce

all day long.   Pick - in' pro - duce all day long.

(Drums fade)

Pick - in' pro - duce all day long.

75

A Quick Picker

Test Drive Your Left Hand...

This tune will separate the 'chords you are learning' from the 'chords you know.' The 'chords you are learning' are the ones you still think about.

The 'chords you know' happen in your hand when you see their names.

Fingerpicking Chords...

We play the first verse with 'thumb and fingers together.' **(42:35)** Beginning with the second verse, we play 'thumb, fingers, thumb, fingers,' like we did in "IN TUNISIA." **(43:02)** If that's too easy... sing along.

Special Effects...

When we started working on this tune, I figured there was no way I would survive the last verse... so I slowed the tape down and prerecorded my part. Of course when we made the recording, we played the tape back at normal speed and I had to keep up with it. I got pretty close, don't you think?

The point is, don't believe everything you see in the movies... unless of course you can do it yourself.

Photo: Melodie Gimple

A QUICK PICKER

DVD CHAPTER 21

by Chet Atkins and John Knowles

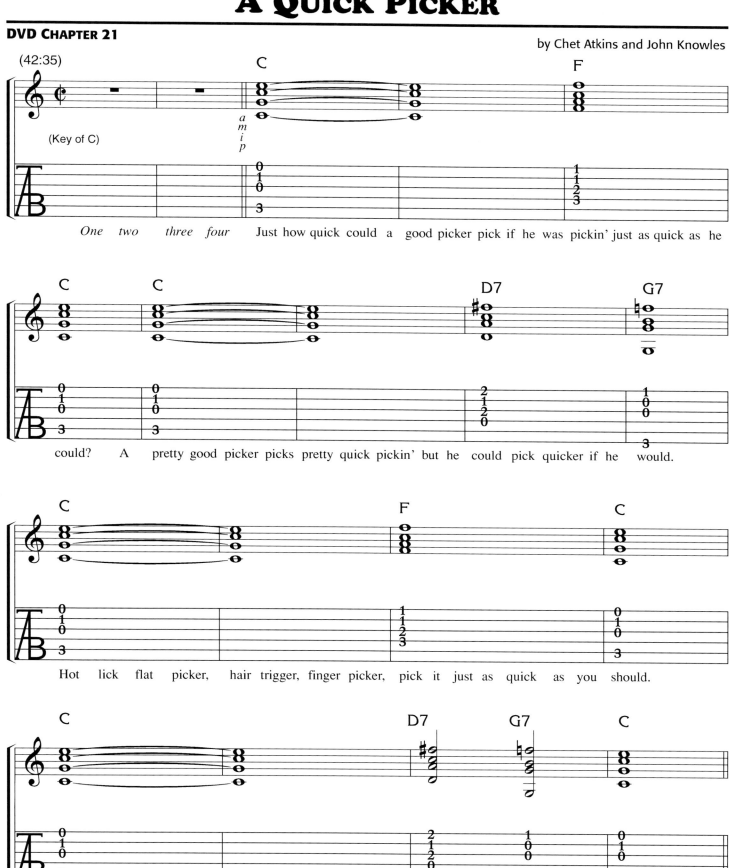

Just how quick could a good picker pick if he was pickin' just as quick as he could? A

pretty good picker picks pretty quick pickin' but he could pick quicker if he would.

Hot lick flat picker, hair trigger, finger picker, pick it just as quick as you should.

Just how quick could a good picker pick if he was pickin' just as quick as he could?

Just how quick could a good picker pick if he was pickin' just as quick as he could? A

pretty good picker picks pretty quick pickin' but he could pick quicker if he would.

81

Hot lick flat picker, hair trigger, finger picker, pick it just as quick as you should.

Just how quick could a good picker pick if he was pickin' just as quick as he could?

KNUCKLEBUSTERS

WARMING UP...

"KNUCKLEBUSTERS" is a set of warm-up exercises that will develop your left hand coordination, your finger independence and your concentration. There are eight exercises... one for each verse of the tune. In the first exercise, each finger moves by itself. Begin by placing your first fingertip on the first string... at the 7th fret. Then place your second, third, and fourth fingertips on the same string at the 8th, 9th, and 10th frets. **(45:16)**

Now lift your first finger... and set it back down. Your right hand is just resting. When you do it to the music, this takes four beats.

LIFT...   SET...
1   2   3   4

This move can be shown on a diagram of the fretboard. A black and white dot (◖) stands for a 'lift and set' (four beats). The first exercise begins with each finger doing a 'lift and set.' Then that group of four moves is repeated.

Now lift your first finger and shift it to the second string... and set it down. The four counts are:

SHIFT...   SET...
1   2   3   4

Each finger shifts to the second string (◯●) (the white dot shows where the finger moves to), and then the fingers move back to the first string.

This one exercise will get you started. After you have learned the moves, turn on the DVD. **(45:50)** Concentrate on moving smoothly with a minimum of effort. I noticed that Elizabeth and Will have a nice way of moving to the music. You can repeat this pattern several times even though they move on to other patterns. You'll know you have it when you can make your moves while you watch them make theirs.

Pattern 1

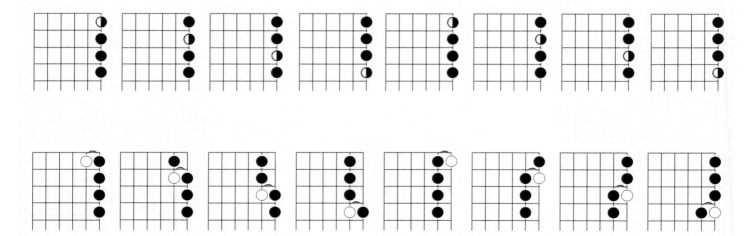

84

ANOTHER KNUCKLEBUSTER...

Here's how to do the second pattern. Start with your fingers on the first string as before. Now 'lift and set' your first finger. Then lift your other three fingers... and set them back down. Those three fingers move like one big finger. Repeat that much. Now are you ready to walk across the neck? First finger... other fingers... first finger... other fingers... The diagrams paint the whole picture. **(46:32)**

Pattern 2

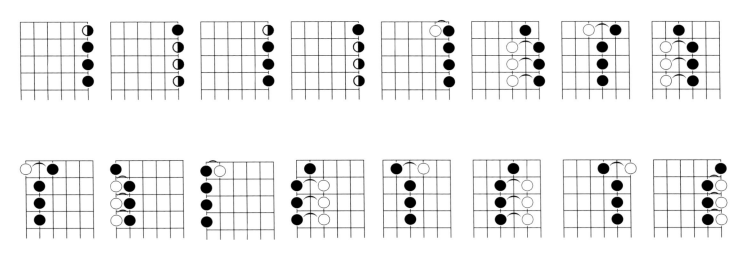

MORE KNUCKLEBUSTER PATTERNS...

The other six patterns are a lot like the second pattern. They just work different combinations of fingers. Each finger gets a chance to work alone... and with the others. Here's how each pattern begins.

Pattern 3 (47:10)

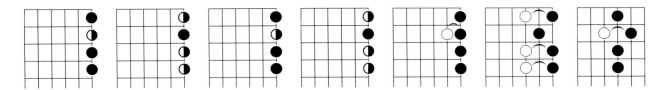

Pattern 4 (47:48)

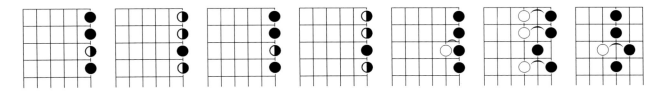

Pattern 5 (48:25)

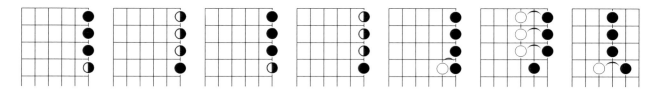

Pattern 6 (49:03)

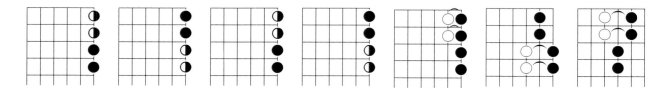

Pattern 7 (49:41)

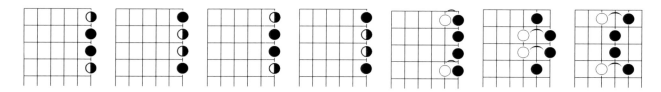

Pattern 8 (50:19)

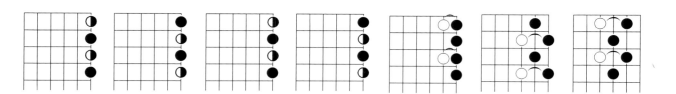

Eventually, you will do all eight combinations. You could even do them all in order.

C7 AND Em7 CHORDS...

The C7 is a C chord with an extra finger. The Em7 is an Em with one less finger. Have you noticed that this same music is playing at the opening and closing of the DVD?

ADDING HARMONY TO MELODY...

Here is a set of chords that I used in my "KNUCKLEBUSTERS" solo. **(49:41)** That first chord is a cousin of the A chord. It looks a little different because I am fingering the first string. You can probably spot the D shape and the F shape. I played some of these chords in other verses with different rhythm patterns. You can experiment with them anywhere in the tune. I did when we recorded it.

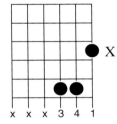

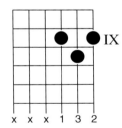

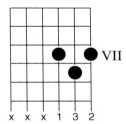

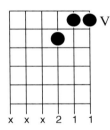

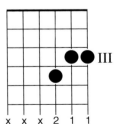

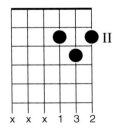

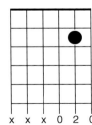

Knucklebusters

by Chet Atkins and John Knowles

One two, one two three four

YANKEE DOODLE DIXIE

DVD CHAPTER 36

If you watch my right hand, you will see that I play "DIXIE" with my fingers and "YANKEE DOODLE" with my thumb. You can practice them separately. The stems on the notes point up for "DIXIE" (♩) and down for "YANKEE DOODLE." (♩) The optional fingering is for those of you who are not used to fretting the bass strings with your left thumb (T).

As you work through this one, listen for "DIXIE"… and then "YANKEE DOODLE." It may help to play it as if it were "DIXIE" with a bass line. You may decide to close your ears and work it out as if it were a lot of two note chords. Once you get it going, sing "DIXIE" as you play both tunes. Then sing "YANKEE DOODLE" while you play.

by Chet Atkins

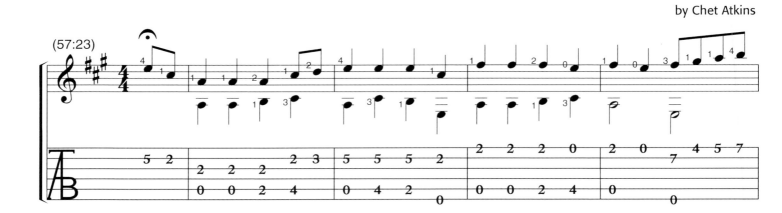

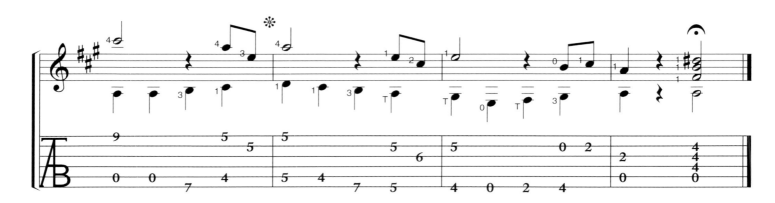

Optional fingering

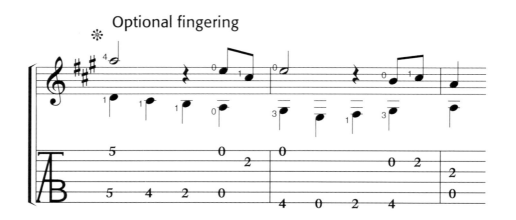

PLAYING CHORDS

The diagrams that guitar players use to learn chords are a simplified picture of the guitar neck. The dots show you where to place your fingertips to play a chord. The numbers are left-hand-finger numbers. An 'o' stands for an open or unfretted string. An 'x' on a string tells you to skip that string when you strum the chord. As you work with these diagrams you will see pictures in your mind and feel shapes in your fingers. You may even hear the sounds of the chords in your imagination.

You will need a dozen or so chords to play all of the songs in the book. These chords are shown below in a pattern that will help you learn to play by ear.

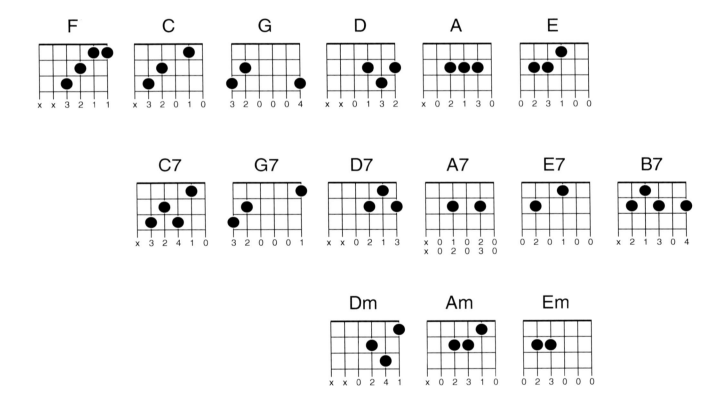

We play a few variations on these basic chords. The diagrams for these are shown below.

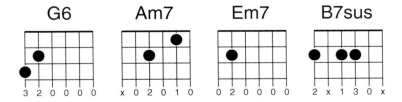

95

Notice the chart position of C and G7… or G and D7. These pairs of chords are used in "JAMBALAYA." You can visualize the chord chart in patterns like these

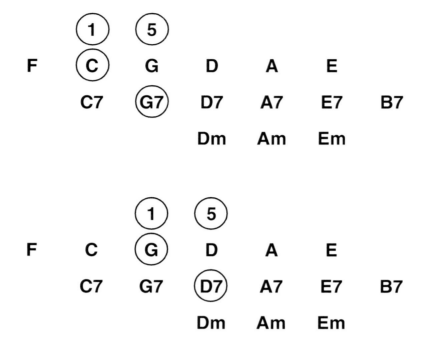

When you play a song, '1' is the key you are in. The other chords are numbered from the 1 chord. If you chose D as 1, which chord would be the 5 chord?

Groups of three chords such as G, C, D7 or D, G, A7 are common to many songs. Check out "ON TOP OF OLD SMOKY." This is called a 1, 4, 5 progression and it looks like this on the chord chart.

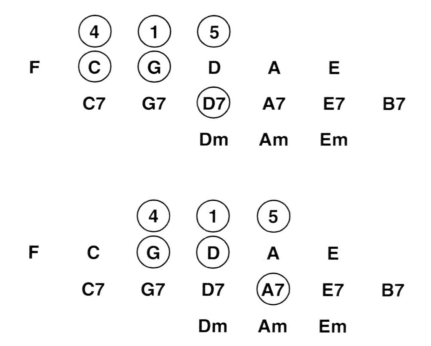

Be on the lookout for patterns like these. The more you play, the more you will see and hear them.

FINGERPICKING CHORDS

As soon as you can play a few chords, you will want to spice up your act with some fancy right-hand moves. We use three basic moves to play all of the backup patterns in the DVD. We'll use the open strings to learn the basic moves and then add the chords.

Begin by placing your right thumb on the fifth string... your index finger on the third string... middle on second... and ring on first. Now keep your fingers in place and sound the fifth string with your thumb several times. You can feel the string spacing in your thumb and fingers.

Now put your thumb back on the fifth string and sound the three treble strings several times. Let your fingers move as a group... and return to the strings as a group. Your hand is basically still because your thumb is in place. Your fingers are doing the moving.

Listen to the sound you are making. Nice sounds come from nice moves. It may be helpful to look in the mirror to see if you look like we do on TV.

Now sound your thumb and fingers together. You will hear four notes. Return to the strings and sound those four notes again. Let your hand be still. Your thumb and fingers make the sound. That is the first basic move.

Here is what it looks like written out in music notation and TAB. The fingers on your right hand are represented by the letters p, i, m, a. Thumb is p... index is i... middle is m... and ring is a. These letters come from the Spanish names for the fingers... pulgar, indicio, medio, and anular.

Place your fingers back on the strings. Sound your thumb... then your fingers... thumb... fingers. That is basic move number two. **(DVD CHAPTER 27)** Basic move number three is thumb... index... middle and ring together... index. **(DVD CHAPTER 29)**

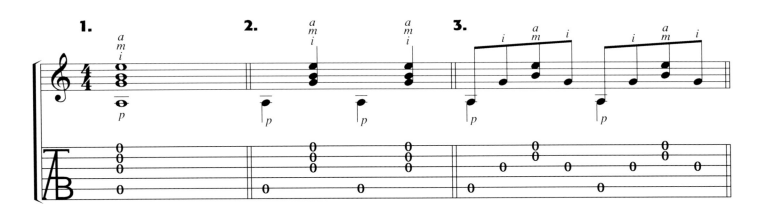

ADDING THE CHORDS...

Now, if you knew which strings to sound with each finger when you played the chords, you'd be all set. Here are some guidelines.

The strongest bass-note for a chord is the chord name. That is, the A chords (A, A7, Am, Am7) sound good with an A bass-note and so forth. Here is a chart that shows the bass string to play for each chord group.

CHORD GROUP	F	C	G	D	A	E	B
BASS STRING	4	5	6	4	5	6	5

So when you play an F chord, your thumb is on the fourth string. That leaves the first, second, and third strings to be sounded by your fingers. When you play a C chord, your thumb sounds the fifth string... and there are four strings left to sound with three fingers.

Most chords will sound good if you play the first three strings with your fingers. Of course you can experiment to find the sound that pleases your ear.

You can practice the first basic move on any song in the DVD. It works like strumming. We used it in the first verse of "QUICK PICKER." (42:35) Here is a sample chord progression that will get you started.

We use the second basic move in "TUNISIA," "JAMBALAYA," "SMOKY" and "QUICK PICKER."

We use the third basic move in "PLAYING FOR SCALE," "YESTERDAY," and "GREENSLEEVES."

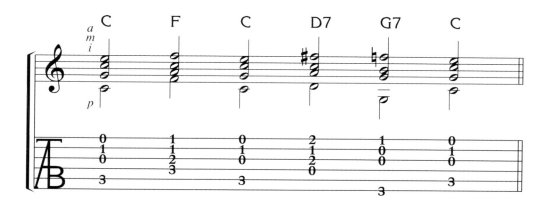

PLAYING MELODIES

As you learn a few chords and play along with the DVD, you will get a feel for how the melodies are played. You will probably rely on some combination of 'playing by ear,' 'reading the music,' and 'watching my hands' to teach yourself to play melodies.

READING MUSIC...

All of the music in this book is written in standard music notation and in tablature (TAB). The two systems work together to show you things like what note to play, where to play it on the guitar, and when to play it.

Here is a sample of music and TAB that shows the notes of the guitar from the low E (sixth string)... to the B at the 19th fret on the first string. I have added the alphabet letter names of the notes so you can begin learning them. Some of you will sit down and memorize all this tonight. Some of you will pick it up as you go along, like remembering friends' phone numbers.

Each line of the TAB stands for one of the six strings of the guitar. The top line represents the first string... and the bottom line represents the sixth string. The numbers are fret numbers. There is a 'G' on the first string at the third fret.

You can find most notes in more than one place on the guitar. You can play an 'A' on the open fifth string and you can play the same 'A' on the sixth string at the fifth fret. You played both A's when you checked your tuning.

The note on the sixth string at the second fret has two names... F sharp (F♯)... and G flat (G♭). It is higher than 'F' and lower than 'G.' Here is a summary of how to play notes that are marked with sharps or flats.

SHARP	(♯)	play one fret higher
FLAT	(♭)	play one fret lower

You may run across a double sharp (×) which means to play that note two frets higher than normal. A natural (♮) means "play the normal note for that measure or until you see a sharp or a flat."

You will learn a lot about the names and the locations of the notes by playing the melody to "PLAYING FOR SCALE." Can you name the notes as you play them... as if the scale tune had lyrics? **(DVD CHAPTER 11)**

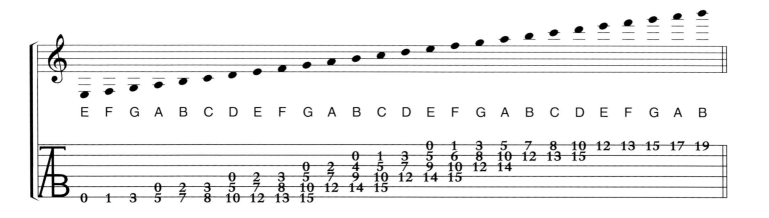

TIMING...

In Will's "GREENSLEEVES" solo, **(DVD CHAPTER 17) (35:42)** the quarter note (♩) gets one beat. You can get a feel for the timing by tapping quarters and following the printed music with your finger as you listen. Then you can examine the chart below that summarizes the time values of the notes.

TIME VALUES OF THE NOTES

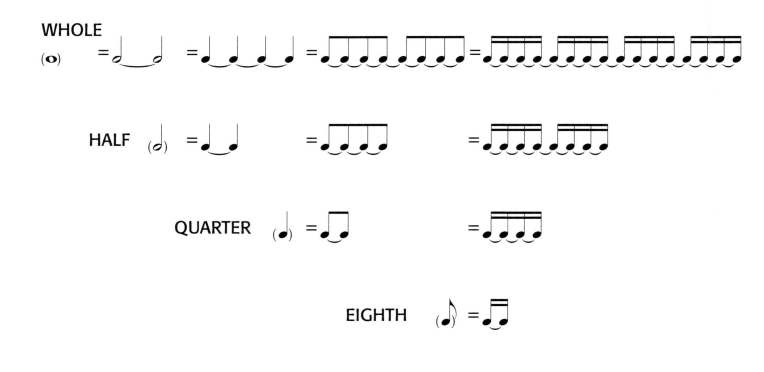

You can look at this chart and see things like, "A whole note gets the same time as two half notes."

The notes can be dotted to alter their time values.

PLAYING BY EAR

Close your eyes and imagine that you are listening to the national anthem. What do you hear? Are there instruments playing? Is anyone singing? Is it a solo, a choir, or a crowd at the ball game? Are there pictures that go with your replay of the national anthem? Maybe you were on the team and you can feel the wooden bench. Open your eyes.

Each one of us has a recording like this that is just waiting to be played back. It's the way our brains work. We learned the national anthem by ear. Some of us sing it better than others but all of us know it.

The first step in learning by ear is to listen and watch over and over.

Have you ever tried reading music by ear? Well, not exactly…but you can learn a lot by listening to the soundtrack while following the printed music.

Choose a tune and cue the DVD. Open the book to the tune and start the DVD. Point to the beginning of the tune and tap your finger as you hear the count.

Some songs have two (¢) or four (4/4) beats in a measure and some have three (3/4). You can tell by looking at the beginning of the piece or by listening to the count. You may notice that songs in 3/4 (waltz) time sound and feel different from the others.

Now tap the beats in each measure as you listen to the music. The object is to get to the end of the printed music at the same time we finish the song on the DVD. Watch for clues like lyrics and ends of verses.

Before long you will be able to follow the music just like following a speech that someone is reading. The music on paper will begin to look like the music you hear. You may even spot something that you missed when you were playing along.

One of the best ways to check what you have learned by ear is to sing along with us. A good place to start is "IN TUNISIA." The more you sing the tuning notes, the easier it will be to tune the guitar.

When I tune, I start with the high E (1st) string and listen to each string going down. **(DVD CHAPTER 2)** You could also check your tuning by listening from the low E (6th) string going up. If you play the low E and then the A (5th) string you will hear the opening notes of "Here Comes the Bride." You can hear the same tune when you play from A to D (5th to 4th) or D to G (4th to 3rd) or B to E (2nd to 1st).

Going from G to B (3rd to 2nd) sounds different. Play the open strings in this order:

D, D, G… D, G, B

Do you recognize the opening notes of "Taps?" Some of you may know it as "Day Is Done." You can play all of "Taps" on these three open strings except for one high note. You can probably find the other note and play the whole tune. **(DVD CHAPTER 24)**

Try playing along with the DVD without looking at the screen or your book. Eventually, you will memorize the whole DVD. But meanwhile, you will prob-

ably drift back and forth between 'playing by ear' and 'playing from memory.'

On a day when you are feeling really loose, you could turn on the DVD and just play along by making things up. All you do is put your fingers on frets and sound the strings. You just might discover something

interesting. It will definitely be original. Your ear taught you where to put your tongue when you were learning to talk. Maybe your ear will teach you where to put your fingers. **(DVD CHAPTER 31)**